SETTLERS IN IRELAND

BRONZE AGE WARRIORS

by
Richard McMinn and
Alan Pinkerton

Illustrations by
Stephen Conlin, B.N. Hartwell and Sharon Heaney

Published by
Stranmillis College
History Department/Learning Resources Unit in
association with The Ulster History Park

Supported by
Department of Education (NI)

Contents

SECTION 1 WHO WERE THE BRONZE AGE SETTLERS ?

SECTION 2 HOW DID BRONZE AGE PEOPLE LIVE ?

SECTION 3 NAVAN

SECTION 4 HOW DID THE BRONZE AGE END ?

Acknowledgements

Typesetting
Deborah Morrison

Design Assistance
Northern Ireland Centre for Learning Resources

Editorial Assistance
Sharon Adams; Michael Avery (Dept. of Archaeology, QUB);
George Beale; Elizabeth Harkin.

ISBN 0 903009 15 3

On a timeline we can go back in time. It can take us from the present to the past. Look at this example:

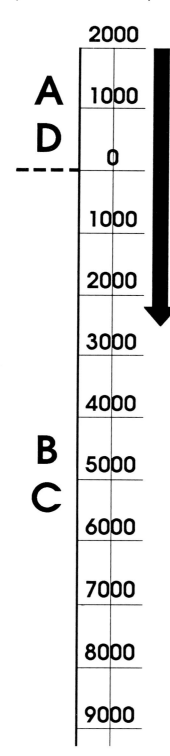

You are here!

If you travel down this timeline you are going BACK in time, back to periods when life was very, very different!

Can you find the year 2500 BC?

The year 2500 BC is very important to us, as it was sometime around then that the Bronze Age started in Ireland. The Bronze Age followed the Neolithic Age, when farming began. The Bronze Age ended around 500 BC.

What was new about the Bronze Age?

Why was it called the Bronze Age?

What is bronze?

Bronze is a metal. It is a mixture of copper and tin. The Bronze Age was when people first began to make and use things made of metal. This was what made it different from earlier times, when people had to use stone tools and weapons.

Why was metal better than stone?

Discuss this with a partner.

ACTIVITY

Copy the heading at the top of page 1 into your workbook and then copy the timeline. Mark the Bronze Age on your timeline and clearly label it.

NEW SETTLERS?

Did new settlers come to Ireland around 2500 BC?

Did these new settlers know how to make metal tools and weapons?

SOME CLUES

A pot or 'beaker' from Largantea, Co. Londonderry.

An arrowhead.

Graves from this time contain a new kind of pot, shaped like a mug or beaker. It has no handles. A new sort of arrowhead has also been found in some of these graves, along with metal objects. Some archaeologists think that these graves are evidence that new settlers arrived in Ireland at this time. These new settlers perhaps brought a knowledge of metal with them. Other archaeologists are not so sure. They think that the people living in Ireland at that time simply copied these things from people in other parts of Europe.

If new people did arrive in Ireland around 2500 BC, where did they come from?

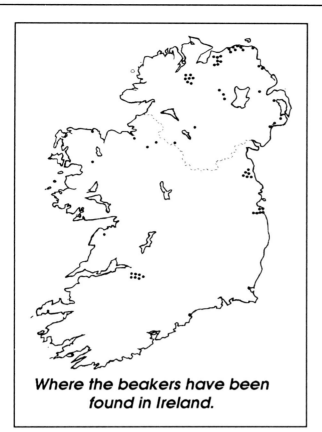

Where the beakers have been found in Ireland.

ACTIVITY

Look at the map carefully. Then answer these questions in your workbook - you may need an atlas to help you.

1. In what part of Ireland have most beakers been found?

2. Where then did the new settlers first land?

3. They probably came from the nearest country. Which country was this?

WHAT WAS BRONZE?

HOW WERE BRONZE OBJECTS MADE?

The first metal objects were made of copper, but it was not very strong or easy to work with. By adding a small amount of tin to copper, people were able to make bronze. This was a harder metal - much better for tools and weapons. The best bronze was made of nine-tenths copper and one-tenth tin.

Where did the copper and tin come from?

Some copper could have been found in the north of Ireland, for example at Conlig, near Bangor, Co. Down. Some tin

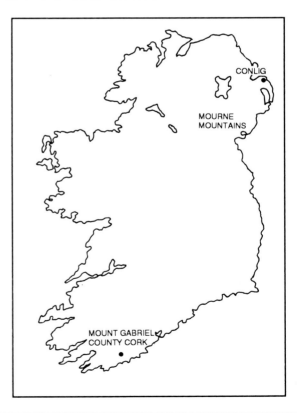

could have been found in the Mourne Mountains. However, much of the copper used in the north may have been brought by traders from County Cork and the tin from Cornwall in England.

What sort of objects were made?

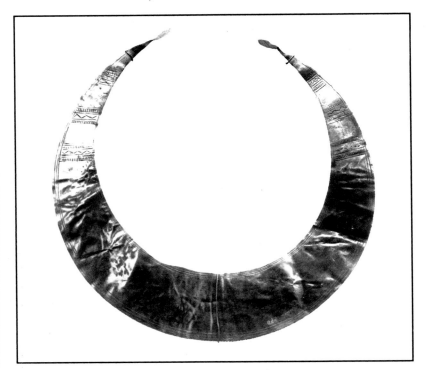

Collars to be worn around the neck (these were made of gold not bronze).

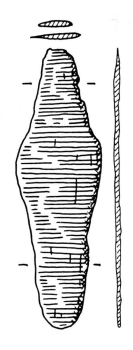

Daggers.

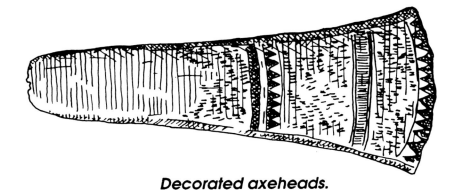

Decorated axeheads.

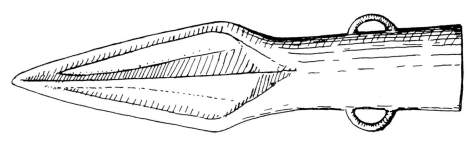

Spears.

THE METAL WORKER

Most people in the Bronze Age were farmers, keeping cattle, sheep, pigs, goats, even horses and growing crops. But the metal worker spent much of his time making things. His hut would have been special and different.

A metal worker's hut.

It would have been circular, with a thatched roof, and a fire in the centre. The fire was used to melt the tin and copper to make bronze. A stone workbench would have had his tools on it - hammers, chisels, tongs, crucibles and moulds. The metal worker is sometimes called a smith

What were crucibles and moulds?

- Crucibles were small clay bowls. They were put in the fire. Into them were placed the tin and copper which then melted.

A stone mould for a flat axehead.

- Moulds were the shapes that the metal workers wanted the finished products to have. At the start of the Bronze Age, they were chiselled out of a piece of stone. The melted metal was poured into the mould to harden. Later it was taken out and hammered into its final shape.

ACTIVITY

In your workbook make drawings of the objects on page 4, along with the hut and the stone mould on this page. Make sure you label each one.

THE METAL WORKER'S APPRENTICE

Here is a story for you to read which tells you much more about the life of a smith or metal worker.

The metal worker was ready to start work but he needed an assistant. He went to a hut and asked one of the boys to become an apprentice. The boy was very proud indeed to have been chosen from all the boys in the small settlement, but he found he had to work very hard.

One day the boy was crouching over the fire in the smith's round hut. Smoke was getting in his eyes, but he could not move away. He had to blow up the fire with a pair of bellows, to keep it glowing. The bellows were made of animal skin, with wooden handles. They had a clay nozzle to poke into the heart of the fire. The boy kept pushing the handles of the bellows up and down as fast as he could.

Propped up in the centre of the fire was a clay crucible. In it was tin and copper, which the smith was melting down into bronze.

The tin and copper had been melted down separately beforehand. The smith had exchanged goods with traders to get what looked like lumps of rock. These had been heated and had changed into shining metal cakes of tin and copper. The bronze-making stage came when the smith put a cake of tin into a crucible with nine times as much copper and asked the boy to melt it down in the fire.

Presently the smith came over and knelt down beside the boy. He jerked his head, and the boy put down the bellows and felt about for the green stick he had brought to the hut that morning. The clay crucible was so hot that the smith could not touch it with his hands. He used a young, green stick so that he could bend it easily round the crucible.

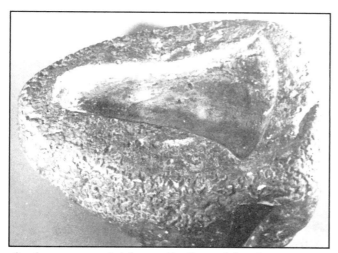

A stone mould from Ballynahinch, Co. Down.

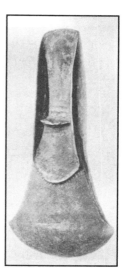

Middle Bronze Age axes.

As the smith bent the stick, the boy moved towards what looked like a pile of flat stones. They were moulds, and were of a type that metal workers had used in the early years of the Bronze Age. Although he now normally used clay moulds, the smith had brought out the old ones to help the boy learn.

The shape of an axe was hollowed out on one side of each stone. The boy blew the dirt out of them and laid several on the floor beside the smith, being careful to see that they were level. Then the smith lifted up the crucible. Very quickly, before the bronze could cool, he poured some into each mould except one. Then he turned to the boy who eagerly took the crucible, heated it up again in the fire, and himself poured the metal into the last mould. The liquid metal is what we today call *molten* metal.

It was the first time that the boy had been allowed to pour out the valuable bronze, and he was very excited. The smith smiled as the boy put down the crucible.

"This is the first axe you have made," he said. "When it is cold, you can try your hand at sharpening it. If you make a good job of it, I will give it to you."

When the boy came to the hut next day, he went straight to the row of moulds. The bronze was now cold and the axes had a dull sheen in the sunshine. He picked up his mould and tipped out the axehead. It was heavy and he rubbed his hand over the smooth, shiny surface.

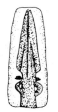

Stone moulds from Killymaddy, Co. Antrim.

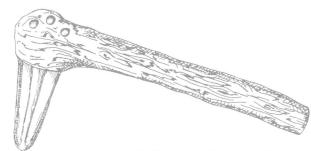

A Bronze Age halberd.

"Now," said the smith. "How do you sharpen these axes?"

The boy looked round for the smith's heavy hammer. Its head was made of a lump of rock, carefully shaped. The boy beat the edge of his bronze axe with it. Under the blows the metal began to spread, especially when he heated the axe in the fire again. He had to do this a number of times. At last, the edge of the blade became thin and sharp.

While the boy was working, the smith had been making a clay mould for a spearhead. He partly buried the mould in the ground to keep it upright. Then he poured in some molten bronze.

When the metal had cooled, the smith broke the clay and took out the shining spearhead. It would fit over the end of a wooden shaft, and be fixed on with two bronze rivets or nails and leather thong binding.

The boy watched, fascinated at what he saw. He was also interested to see the swords and the large bronze cauldron, or cooking pot, that the smith had recently completed. It had taken him many hours of work to produce the fine vessel that would eventually be used in one of the huts. The boy also heard of the bronze trumpets that had been made elsewhere in the country. The boy had only one wish and that was to be a metal worker one day!

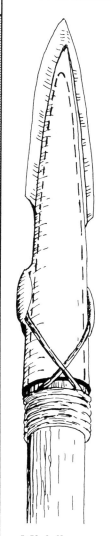

Sheet bronze cauldron from Lisdromturk, Co. Monaghan - perhaps used in preparing feasts.

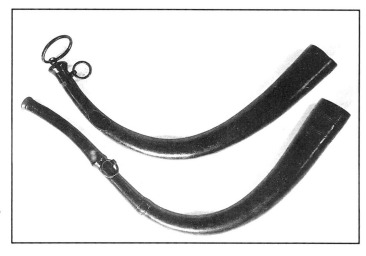

Middle Bronze Age spear fixed to a wooden shaft with binding.

Bronze horns.

Middle Bronze Age spear with holes for leather thongs to fix it to a shaft.

Can you make a mould?

Your class, in groups, might like to try to make clay objects, using moulds.

ACTIVITY

In your workbook, make a series of drawings based on the story of the metal worker's apprentice to show the different stages in making a bronze axe. Label each drawing clearly.

SECTION 2
HOW DID BRONZE AGE PEOPLE LIVE ?

WHAT WERE BRONZE AGE HOUSES LIKE?

Perhaps they were like the one in the drawing below. Archaeologists, however, think this particular building may only have been used as a temporary place to stay while on a hunting trip.

Drawing of a 'hunting lodge' at Cullyhanna Lough, Co. Armagh.

Note:

- the outer oak fence;
- the wooden hut with the thatched roof and chimney;
- the open air cooking place;
- the hunter and the meat hung up to dry.

HOW DID BRONZE AGE PEOPLE COOK THEIR FOOD?

How does your mother or father cook meat for your dinner?

How would you have done this if you had lived in one of the Bronze Age houses at Ballycroghan, near Bangor, Co. Down, about 700 BC?

THINK HARD!
Here are some clues to help you.
You would have used:

- stones - lots of them;
- a wooden shovel;
- water;
- straw;

- wooden planks;
- fire;
- a pit dug in the ground;
- meat.

The cooking would have been done outside in the open air. Kitchens didn't exist then. At Ballycroghan the cooking place was near a river. Can you work out how Bronze Age people cooked their food? Why did they often do this near a river? The next activity will help you.

Bronze Age cooking at the Ulster History Park.

ACTIVITY

BRONZE AGE COOKING

The sentences which follow give all the instructions needed to try out some Bronze Age cooking. One archaeologist in Ireland, Professor M.J. O'Kelly, cooked a large piece of mutton this way. The only problem is that the sentences have been mixed up. Rearrange them and copy them into your workbook under the title:

BRONZE AGE COOKING

1.   dug be A pit would.

2.   planks wooden of the pit The bottom lined would be with.

3.   in poured be which would water The would to hold have trough.

4.   river This might come water a from nearby.

5.   them around built mound piled stones The be would a in and a fire.

6.   lit fire would be The in put stones more and.

7.   trough be and then would into the shovelled an hour After about be would stones red-hot the.

8.   boil water the Eventually would meat, wrapped in straw, and the would in dropped be cook to.

9.   added be would stones hot More ready was meat the until.

HOW DID RICH PEOPLE LIVE IN THE BRONZE AGE?

For the first time some people became rich during the Bronze Age. The rich were the leaders who did not have to work as farmers or as smiths. Archaeologists have found some clues about their lives. We can now work out what they wore and how they passed their time.

What did rich men wear and how did they appear?

CLUES

Bronze ring from Seacon More, Ballymoney, Co. Antrim.

Bracelet from Downpatrick, Co Down.

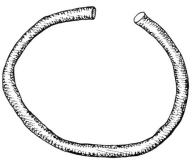

Collar worn around the neck from Largatreany, Co. Donegal.

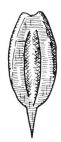

Razor.

Gold cloak fastener from Lattoon, Co. Cavan.

Razor from Killevy, Co. Armagh.

A man's costume from Late Bronze Age Denmark.

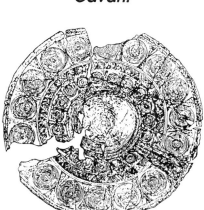

Cloak fastener from Lattoon, Co. Cavan.

Bronze pin to fasten a cloak from Derryhale, Co. Armagh.

How did rich men pass their time?

ACTIVITY

In your workbook, write some sentences describing what a rich man looked like in the Bronze Age and how he passed his time. Then make a drawing of a Late Bronze Age Warrior.

CLUES

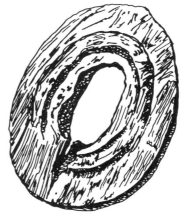

Shield mould from Kilmahamogue, Co. Antrim.

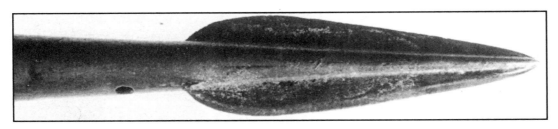

Late Bronze Age spear (note hole for rivet to fasten it to a wooden shaft).

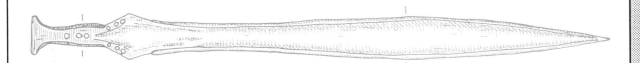

Late Bronze Age sword from Inishowen, Co. Donegal.

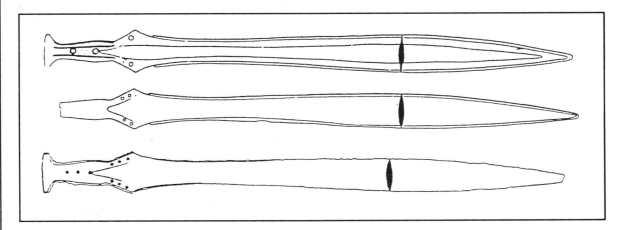

The Ballycroghan swords (now in Bangor Heritage Centre) - Late Bronze Age.

BURYING THE DEAD

In the Bronze Age most people died before they reached the age of 35. Life was short. The bodies of the dead were no longer buried in large stone tombs like those built by the Neolithic farmers. Instead, they were usually burnt and the ashes put in a small, simple grave called a CIST (pronounced KIST). This was made by digging a hole in the ground and then putting in four stone "walls". One or two clay pots, or even a dagger or some metal tools, were often also put in the grave. A large stone was placed over the grave. Sometimes these graves were made beside each other to form a cemetery.

The stone "walls" of a cist grave.

A stone cist grave for one person (notice the handmade clay pot).

MYSTERIOUS STANDING STONES AND STONE CIRCLES

Bronze Age people may not have built large stone tombs, but they did put up large standing stones, possibly beside the graves of the dead. Archaeologists aren't sure about this. They are also puzzled by mysterious circles of stones, built in the Bronze Age. Two examples are shown on the next page.

Standing stone at Ballybeen, Dundonald, Co. Down.

What were these stone circles used for?

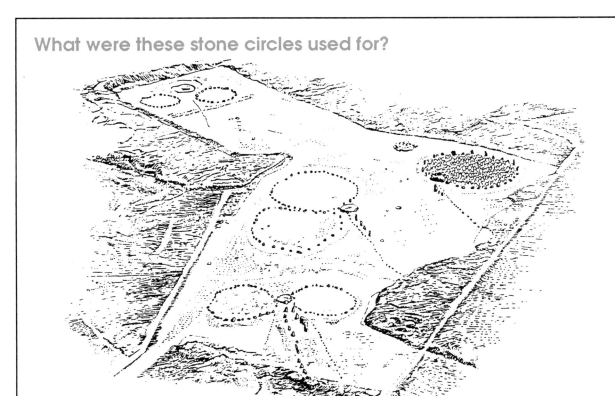

Bird's-eye view of the stone circles at Beaghmore, Co. Tyrone.

Beltany stone circle, Co. Donegal.

Discuss this with a partner. Here are some possibilities to help you:

- burial places;
- places for great ceremonies;
- places for observing the sun and the stars.

THE STORY OF NAVAN IN THE BRONZE AGE

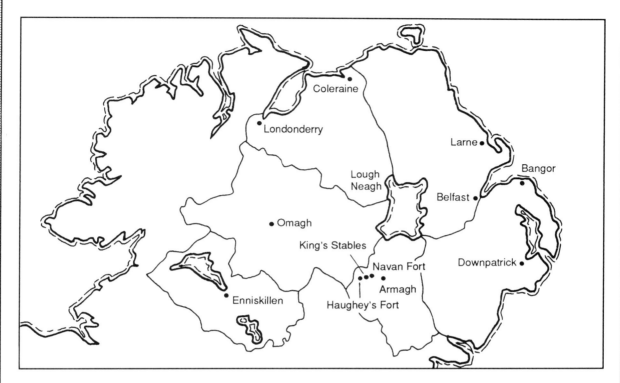

The location of Navan Fort, outside Armagh, Co. Armagh.

Here is a story for you to read about a visit by a boy and a girl to Navan in the late Bronze Age. The story will tell you about what life was like in Ulster at that time.

The boy and his sister were very excited. Their father had promised to take them to visit the King's great house. They had hardly been able to sleep the night before. They had never gone on such a journey.

They set off early in the morning to walk from their home to the great hill some miles away. As they got nearer, they could see smoke rising from all the fires on the hill-top. They soon realised that there were many huts and other buildings on the hill and all around it. This was amazing. So many people and so many animals! As they came closer to the main hill, their father explained that the King was a very important man and that he was holding a huge feast that evening for his people. They were all invited!

To reach the King's house on the top of the hill, they first had to cross a huge bank of earth and beyond it a deep ditch. As they scrambled across the ditch, the boy was puzzled.

Navan Fort today. You can see the outer bank and ditch clearly, as well as the site of the palace (the larger mound with the trees around it).

The hut at the top of the hill. You can also see the ditch which enclosed the site, the fencing which kept the animals in, the crops and the entrance causeway, or bridge, over the ditch on the eastern side.

"Father", he asked, "why are the bank and ditch the wrong way round?"

"What do you mean?"

"Well," said the boy, "surely, if the King's house is attacked, it would be difficult to defend. The attackers would be able to climb up to the top of the bank. Then they could throw spears down on the defenders on the far side of the ditch below."

"You're quite right", said his father. "The King's house is not meant to be a proper fort. It is a place for ceremonies and feasting. If a war begins, the King and his family can move to the proper fort, which is only a short distance away. It has three huge ditches defending it, as well as a wooden fence or stockade around its buildings. The ditches are so deep and wide, the King would be safe there. I'll take you to see it tomorrow."

Haughey's Fort. You can see the three ditches protecting it clearly. It is three-quarters of a mile west of Navan Fort.

They plodded on up the hill towards the King's house. They could feel the sun on their backs as they approached the entrance on the eastern side of the inner enclosure. They hadn't seen the sun very often recently. The weather had been very bad, with lots of rain. Many of the crops had been ruined and some people were starving. They crossed the causeway with its wooden fencing on either side. They stopped to admire the cattle, sheep, goats and pigs, grazing in the enclosure. Their father explained that the King's animals were bigger in size than everybody else's, because they were so well fed. Often, he said, the Kings and Queens of Ireland had arguments about who had the biggest bulls. These arguments could sometimes lead to war.

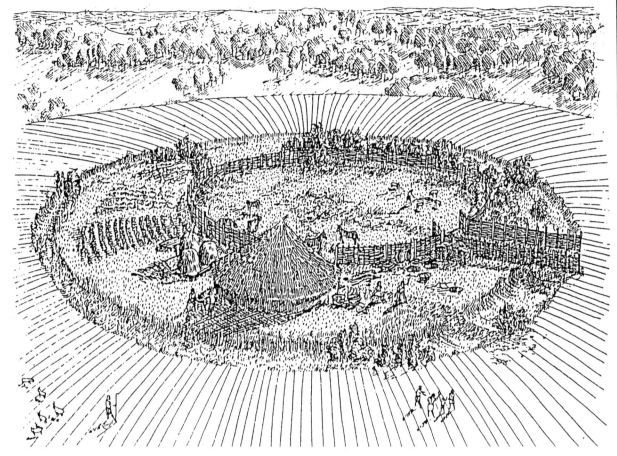

Navan Fort - the royal enclosure.

Outside the King's hut his horses grazed and his big hunting dogs played with each other in the sunshine. In a cage at the entrance to the hut was an amazing sight. The children had never seen anything like it before.

"What is it?", they asked.

"Oh", said their father, "it is a strange animal from a place far away across the sea. It is an ape. Traders brought it on their ship as a gift to the King. Some people say the King of another land sent it to our King as a present."

That night the King held a great feast. The children watched from the entrance of the hut. The King and his friends, including their father, had roasted pig to eat as a special treat. The children fell asleep around a fire outside.

Next morning, their father took them over to visit the nearby fort, as he had promised. As they crossed the third and last ditch of the fort, the smell was awful. This was the toilet for the soldiers and their families. No doubt about that.

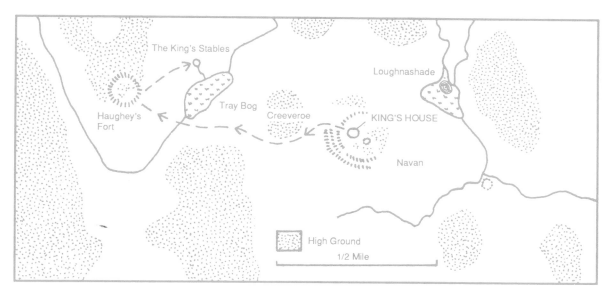

The children's route from the King's house to the fort and then to the pool.

Within the fort there was much to see. Inside several huts metal workers were busy making swords and gold objects. Outside women were grinding corn and looking after the fires in the cooking pits. The children and their father then walked on to the bottom of the hill beyond the fort. A small crowd had gathered around a pool of water. As they got closer, the children became frightened. The crowd began to chant strange words. Then the King gave an order. Some swords were thrown into the pool. Next, a red deer and a dog were thrown into the water. Both were already dead.

"Father, why is this happening?", the children asked in worried voices.

"These are sacrifices to the gods. The King wants them to stop all this rain. The crops need better weather. Tomorrow, a young man will be killed and part of his head thrown into the pool."

Modern children visit the pool, now called The King's Stables.

The children felt glad that they would not be there to see this. As they walked home that afternoon, the sky grew dark. Big drops of rain began to fall. The gods did not seem to be listening.

WHAT THE ARCHAEOLOGISTS FOUND AT NAVAN

How do we know what happened in the story is correct?

When the archaeologists excavated the sites at Navan, they found some interesting clues. First they had to remove the top layers of soil.

At the palace or Navan Fort they found the following:

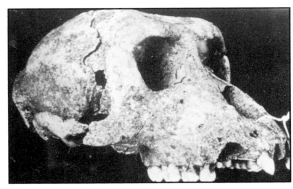

The skull of a North African ape.

At Haughey's Fort they found:

The skull of a very large dog (the one on the left of the photograph).

Animal bones and parts of wooden tools at the bottom of the inner ditch.

The remains of cooking pits and a wooden fence or stockade inside the fort.

The third or inner ditch, with evidence of its use as a toilet.

At the pool known as The King's Stables they found:

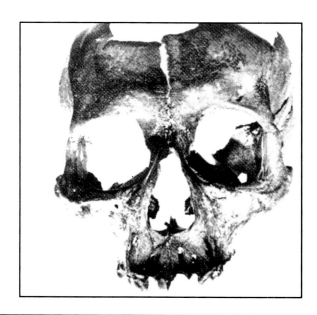

The skull of a young man whose face had been cut off from the rest of his head.

ACTIVITY

Here are some questions about the story of the children's visit to Navan. Answer them in your workbook.

1. What modern city is close to Navan?

2. How do we know that Navan Fort was not really a proper fort?

3. What was the weather like around 500 BC?

4. Why were the King's animals bigger than everyone else's?

5. Why did the Kings and Queens of Ireland sometimes go to war with each other?

6. Archaeologists found the skull of a strange animal at Navan which proved that the hill must have been the home of a king or great chief. What was this animal and where had it come from? How had it got to Ireland?

7. What special food was eaten at feasts?

8. What did the people of the nearby Haughey's Fort use as their toilet?

9. How do we know Haughey's Fort was a real fort?

10. What did archaeologists find evidence of inside Haughey's Fort?

11. What is the special pool called today?

12. What did people do at the special pool in the Late Bronze Age? Why did they do this?

HOW DID THE BRONZE AGE END ?

A STRANGE MYSTERY

Archaeologists don't really know how or why the Bronze Age ended. They are not even sure when it happened. By about 300 BC iron tools and weapons, such as a new kind of sword, began to appear in Ireland. These swords often had beautiful scabbards to hold them. Similar swords and scabbards have been found across the sea in other parts of Europe.

Was Ireland invaded by new settlers?

Not many iron objects from this time have been found. But then iron does not keep as well as bronze or gold, if it is lying underground. Iron becomes rusty and disappears. Archaeologists have also found some clues about the weather at this time. They think it may have been very bad. A lot of rain may have fallen. If so, the crops would have been damaged. Many people would have had no food.

Why did the Bronze Age end?

Discuss this with a partner. Use the clues mentioned on this page to help you. Perhaps we will never know for sure.

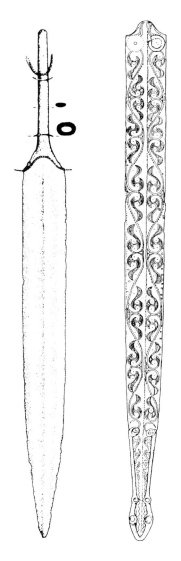

Left - Lisnacrogher iron sword (Co. Antrim).

Right - Scabbard for Lisnacrogher sword.

ACTIVITY

1. Copy the drawings of the iron sword and scabbard on this page into your workbook.

2. Try putting an iron nail in some water to see how quickly it rusts.

WORDSQUARE

You have been reading about, writing about and discussing how we know about the Bronze Age people who lived in Ireland long before us. Now have some fun with this word square. First of all copy it into your workbook. Then try to find the hidden words. They are all used somewhere in this book. When you find a word, draw a circle around it in your workbook. An example has been done for you. There are 40 hidden words to find.

B	R	O	N	Z	E	C	O	P	P	E	R
E	A	P	E	T	U	A	S	I	A	X	E
A	Z	O	D	Z	I	U	K	N	L	M	C
K	O	R	B	U	L	L	U	B	A	O	R
E	R	K	B	C	C	D	L	A	C	U	U
R	I	V	E	T	A	R	L	N	E	L	C
D	C	X	E	F	Z	O	G	K	X	D	!
I	L	C	I	R	O	N	A	V	A	N	B
T	O	I	Z	M	E	T	A	L	G	H	L
C	A	S	X	S	H	I	E	L	D	T	E
H	K	T	D	O	G	N	S	M	I	T	H
C	A	U	S	E	W	A	Y	M	S	S	M
O	R	A	C	B	E	L	L	O	W	S	O
L	R	B	L	M	I	N	E	U	O	P	L
L	O	D	A	G	G	E	R	N	R	E	T
A	W	Q	Y	F	O	R	T	D	D	A	E
R	S	C	A	B	B	A	R	D	P	R	N

ACKNOWLEDGEMENTS

The publishers wish to thank the following for their kind permission to reproduce illustrations.

J.P. Mallory and T.E. McNeill for the photographs on the cover, and pages 7 (left), 9 (centre), 15, 16, 18, 19, 22 (top) and 23, and the drawings on the frontispiece and pages 2 (top), 4, 8 (left), 9, 10, 13 (all except bottom left), 14 (except the Ballycroghan swords), 18, 20 and 25, and the maps on pages 3 and 21.

Bangor Heritage Centre for the drawing of the Ballycroghan swords on page 14.

E. Brennan for the drawings on pages 8 (right) and 13 (bottom left).

QUB Archaeological Teaching Collection for the photographs on pages 7 (right & centre), 9 (right) and 14, and the drawing on page 2 (bottom).

Environment Service: Historic Monuments and Buildings, for the photograph on page 22 (bottom) and the drawing on page 16. Crown copyright reserved.

The Trustees of the Ulster Museum for the photograph on page 4.

The Ulster History Park for the photograph on page 11.